Sophie loves adventures and playing with her best friend Nick, but one day Mum and Dad tell her that they have to move to a new city...

Sophie is a little girl who happily plunges into every new adventure. She likes dressing up because she can be anything she wants to be: a magician, a construction worker, a pirate, or a beautiful fairy.

Sophie has many friends, but she mostly plays with Nick, her best friend from next door.

They spend a lot of time together having dance parties in the kitchen, making sandcastles at the beach or searching for fairies in the garden.

But one day Mum and Dad wanted to talk to her about something important, and she became nervous.

Hearing the words 'new city', 'new friends' and 'moving,' Sophie felt like she was on a plane, falling down straight towards the ground.

The little girl tried to convince her parents not to move, but she quickly learned that it wasn't an option.

'Listen, Sophie, I got a new job in another city. We know moving is a big change for you, and we know you will miss Nick and the kids from school terribly', Dad said.

'But the good news is that there will be loads of kids in our new neighbourhood. We are sure you will make new friends easily. And when you feel sad, we can always phone Nick and speak to him.'

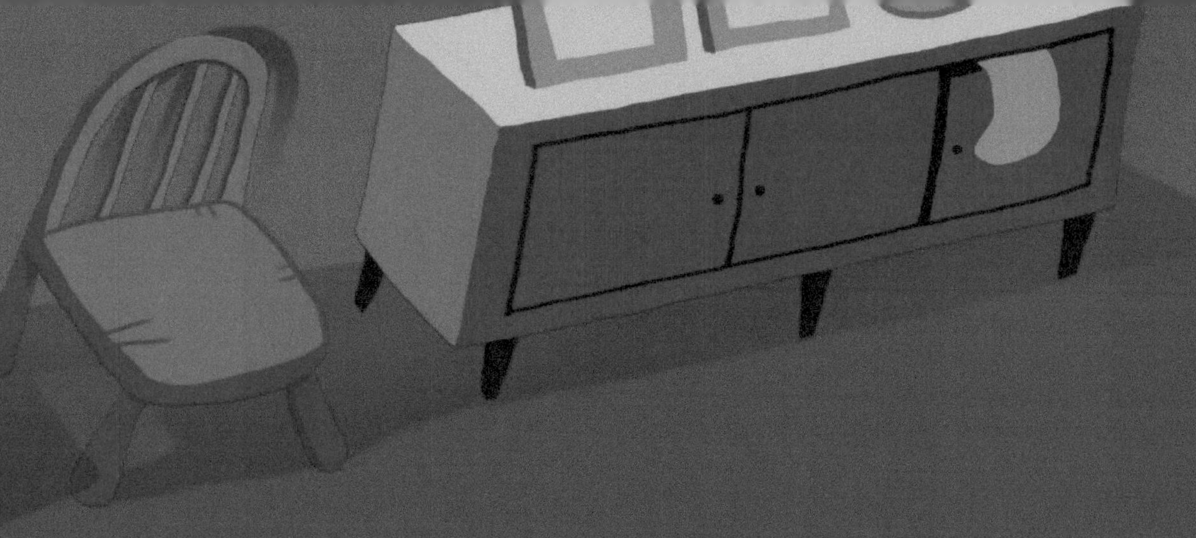

Over the next few days, it was difficult for Sophie to eat, sleep, or listen to anything anyone said.

She just hugged her plush T-Rex Dino and snuggled up in her bed under the covers.

'What am I going to do, Dino? All my friends are here.' Sophie cried.

'It's okay, Sophie. You'll miss your friends, but you'll find new ones. Plus, I'll be there with you.

Take me with you everywhere you go in the new city and when you look at me, remember that everything will be okay.

I'll be there to protect you and keep you company', Dino said.

On moving day, Mum and Dad organised a farewell party for Sophie, so she could say goodbye to everyone and especially Nick.

'Here Sophie, I have a picture for you, so you won't forget me. I will come and visit you soon', Nick said and gave Sophie a big hug.

On the first day in the new city, Sophie was sorrowful. The little girl missed everything and everyone from her old life.

While her Mum and Dad carried the heavy boxes into the new house, Sophie sat on the front steps with Dino.

Seeing all the kids playing in the street, Sophie felt miserable. She put both of her hands on her stomach and pressed down. This funny feeling she felt in her belly just wouldn't go away.

'Does your tummy hurt?' asked the girl from next door, as she sat down next to Sophie.

'Yes... no... I don't know.' Sophie was unsure how to describe the funny feelings inside her body.

I know,' she said. 'Don't worry, it will get better.'

'Really?' Sophie turned to look at her.

'Yes! When I first moved here, I felt alone too, but after a while, I met all the kids in the neighbourhood, and made new friends.'

Sophie could feel her tummy get better. She stopped pressing on it and lifted her head up high.

'I'm Anne. Come on, I'll introduce you to everyone,' she said.

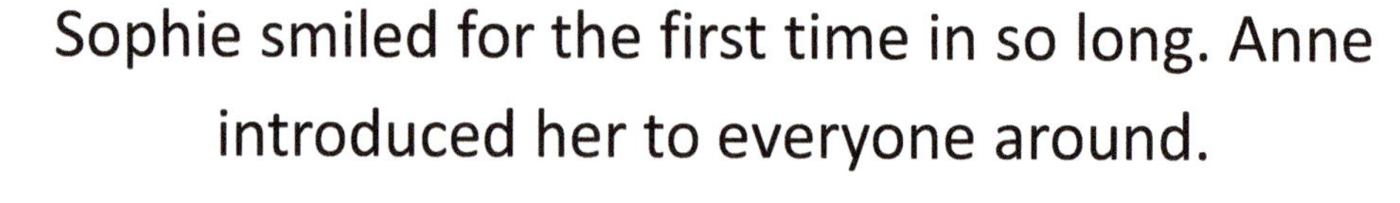

Sophie smiled for the first time in so long. Anne introduced her to everyone around.

That day, Sophie got to know her new neighbours a little better, one by one. There were a ton of kids her age on her street.

The other kids invited Sophie to join in their treasure hunt, and from one moment to the next, she was on a big ship looking through a telescope. 'There is the island, Dino,' Sophie shouted excitedly.

Soon after they reached the island, they searched for the treasure.

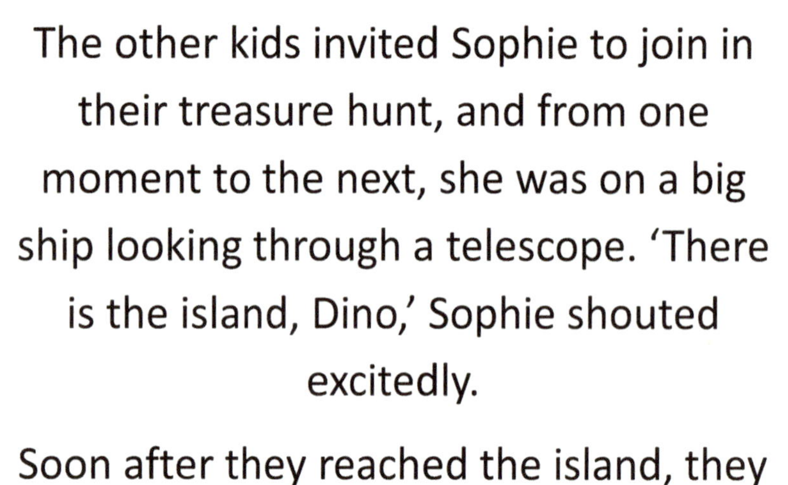

Suddenly she heard her name:
'Soooophie'! It was Mum, and dinner
was ready.

'No Mum, I can't leave the island yet,
we are still looking for the treasure.'

'Ok, but please come straight home
once you have found it,' Mum said.

Of course, Sophie hadn't forgotten about her old life.
And when she was lying in bed that night, she cuddled
up to Dino and called Nick.

'It's so nice to see you, Nick! I hope you'll come soon
and visit us,' Sophie said with a warm smile on her face.

Quickly, she realised that with Dino and Anne
by her side, she would never be alone or
scared.

In fact, she was ready to give her new city a good go and welcome all the new adventures.